WILD CATS

ISBN 0-590-40741-4

Copyright © 1986 by Ilex Publishers Limited
Illustrated by Jim Channell / Linden Artists
All rights reserved. Published by
Scholastic Inc., 730 Broadway, New York, NY 10003
by arrangement with Ilex Publishers Limited

12 11 10 9 8 7 6 5 4 3 2 1   7 8 9/8 0 1 2/9

Printed in Italy

First Scholastic printing: February 1987

WILD CATS

Written by Mark Carwardine
Illustrated by Jim Channell

SCHOLASTIC INC.
New York Toronto London Auckland Sydney

This series is dedicated to Georgia, aged 7 who
showed us how children look at animals

CONTENTS

Cats arranged by geographical location

Lion

A lion's roar can be heard as far away as five miles. It is used to frighten off neighboring lions and to tell members of its family where it is hiding.

Lions nearly always live in groups, or prides. Sometimes there may be as many as twenty-five of them living together in one place.

About two hundred lions live in a forest in India, but most live on the grassy plains and in the open woodlands of Africa.

Lions eat many kinds of other animals, including wildebeest, zebras, giraffes, buffalos and warthogs. Because they cannot run as fast as many of these animals, they have to creep up on their prey, or hide and then pounce on them. Sometimes they eat mice, rabbits, small birds, snakes and lizards as well. The females do most of the hunting; the male's mane makes him too easy to see, so his chief role in the pride is to defend it from intruders.

Most lions spend the day sleeping in the shade to escape the heat of the

African sun. Sometimes they even rest on a branch in a tree. Lion cubs, however, are very lively. They spend most of their time playing games with the other cubs in the pride.

Cheetah

The cheetah is the fastest runner on earth. It can reach speeds of over sixty miles an hour and can accelerate from zero to fifty in just a few seconds.

It stalks animals such as gazelles and impala until it is about three hundred feet away from a likely victim. Then it suddenly sprints forward making incredibly sudden and sharp turns in hot pursuit of its prey. But cheetahs tire very quickly and can only run at top speed for very short distances – so most chases are unsuccessful – and the animals get away.

Unlike most other cats, cheetahs are active during the day. They live in the semi-desert and open grassland areas of Africa and a few parts of Asia. They like to perch on high places – their keen eyesight enables them to see long distances if they sit on a fallen tree, a hilltop or a termite mound.

Young cheetahs can be born in almost any month of the year. They spend most of their time in a carefully-concealed den but, if danger threatens, their mother carries them in her mouth to a safer hiding place. They often huddle close to her for

protection from enemies or for shade from the tropical sun. When about six weeks old they begin to follow her around, learning to hunt in preparation for leaving home in about a year's time.

Serval

Porcupines are not the only animals that live in porcupine burrows. A beautiful cat, the serval, often makes its home in them as well. It uses the burrows to hide in and as a home in which to rear its young.

As many as four kittens are born in a burrow, or in another suitable hiding place, where they are safely out of sight. If danger threatens, their mother moves them to a new den, carrying them one at a time in her mouth. There they stay until they are old enough to join her on hunting trips, to learn the skills they will need to catch food later in life.

Servals are found in Morocco, Algeria and most of Africa south of the Sahara desert. They live in savanna grasslands, along with elephants, rhinos, lions and all the other well-known animals of Africa. Although they can be found almost anywhere, they prefer places where there is plenty of water, such as near a stream or lake.

Servals hunt alone, nearly always after dark. They often move up to two or three miles in a single night. Hunting mostly by sound, they search for snakes, rats, mice and voles in the long grass. Their enormous ears enable them to pick up every chirp, squeak and rustle nearby, before they pounce on their unsuspecting prey with a swift leap. In the daytime, they also sometimes hunt small birds. They can even capture them in flight — with remarkable leaps of up to ten feet into the air.

Caracal

Caracals have often been trained by people in India and Iran to stalk and catch animals like hares, peacocks, crows and cranes. They are very fast cats and jump remarkably well, so make efficient and willing hunters.

In the wild they hunt mostly at night, or in the morning and evening, depending on how hot it has been during the day. Caracals do not like heat, so in summer they are almost entirely night animals. Only during colder weather can they be seen trotting along a bush road or path in broad daylight.

Found throughout most of Africa, across the Arabian peninsula and as far east as north-western India, caracals feed mainly on small deer and antelope, such as klipspringers. Sometimes they drag their kill up into the fork of a tree, where it can be eaten at leisure without being disturbed by jackals, hyenas and other predators.

Young caracals are fully-finished miniatures of their parents, with tawny coats and black, pointed ears. They can move their ears around to show whether they are feeling cross, frightened or mischievous. When only four or five weeks old they are already very lively, tearing around with great speed and romping playfully with each other. They remain with their mother for about a year, before moving on to find a new home in a woodland or scrubby area nearby.

Sand cat

The sand cat, which lives in deserts, has thick fur on the bottom of its feet specially to help it walk over the hot sand without getting burned. This valuable padding also keeps it from sinking as it wanders over the soft dunes.

Sand cats are found in many parts of North Africa and as far east as Pakistan and other parts of Asia. They even live in the Sahara Desert, where it is so hot during the day that they have to hide in a sandy hole or

between rocks to keep out of the sun. They hunt mostly at night, or in the evening and early morning, when it is cooler and they can safely come out in the open. Their enormous eyes help them see in the dark and their very keen hearing helps to detect likely prey. They eat mostly jerboas, sand voles and other small rodents, though occasionally they catch hares, birds, snakes, lizards and locusts. Perhaps surprisingly, they never have to drink but get enough moisture from their food.

Sand cats have to keep their eyes and ears open for enemies such as eagles, buzzards, poisonous snakes and wolves. They are able to flatten themselves close to the ground to hide if they detect one of these dangerous animals nearby.

Tiger

Only a century ago there were a hundred thousand tigers living all over Asia. They prowled jungles, woodlands, swamps and grasslands wherever there was enough water, food and places to hide.

But today there are only a few thousand tigers left. All the others have been shot, trapped or poisoned by people. Only in the last few years, since there have been special laws to protect them and tiger reserves where they can live in safety, have their numbers started to increase once again.

Tigers are the largest members of the cat family. But their sizes vary according to where they live. The farther north they come from the bigger they are; the Siberian tiger is the biggest of all.

Tigers spend most of the daytime resting in the shade under a tree or lying in a quiet pool of water, to escape the heat of the midday sun. As soon as it starts to get dark they go out hunting. Tigers can see and hear extremely well and their stripes enable them to hide unseen in the tall grass. Usually, they look for deer, wild cattle or wild pigs but they will eat whatever they can catch — including baby elephants or rhinos — and even people. Man-eating, though, is very rare and most tigers prefer to avoid meeting people if they possibly can.

Snow leopard

The snow leopard is an exceptionally beautiful cat with long, silky fur. It is closely-related to the true leopard and is similar in size and shape. But it does not roar like other cats, more commonly making a loud, eerie moaning call.

Snow leopards are very rare animals, because many of them have been hunted for their attractive spotted coats. But they can still be found in some of the high mountains of central Asia, where they are very graceful and agile in moving over the difficult ground. One has even been seen jumping as far as fifty feet from one rock to another.

They sleep at night and in the middle of the day, usually in rocky caverns or crevices in the mountains. During the early morning and late afternoon, though, they are very active and roam widely looking for food. Snow leopards eat all kinds of other animals, including mountain goats, sheep,

deer, wild boar, marmots and pikas. In winter, they have to move from the high, treeless mountain slopes when the prey animals go to live in the warmer forests.

Young snow leopards are born in the summer, from April to June. They stay hidden inside a rocky shelter, lined with their mother's fur, until about three months old. Then they cautiously emerge to see the outside world for the first time, always staying close by their mother's side. After about a year they leave for good and begin to wander the mountains alone in search of a new home.

Fishing cat

Most cats do not like water. But the fishing cat often spends hours paddling in rivers and lakes. It is even quite happy to swim in deep water and sometimes dives under the surface. Its fingers and toes have slight webbing between them – just like those of a duck – to help it swim more easily.

Fishing cats live in many parts of Asia, including islands such as Sri Lanka, Sumatra and Java. They make their homes in marshes,

it up, or they pin it to the stream bed. If they have a bad day's fishing, they will also hunt for shrimps, crabs, snails, frogs, snakes, birds and mice.

Fishing cats are considerably larger than pet cats. Their fur is short and rough, and their tails are extremely thick. The kittens, however, which are born in April or May, do not grow as big as their parents until they are at least nine months old.

mangrove swamps and along creeks and rivers. Every day they patiently and quietly crouch on a rock or sand bank, waiting for a fish to swim nearby. As soon as one does, they quickly use a paw as a fishing net to scoop

Jungle cat

The jungle cat stalks its prey skillfully and quietly. As soon as it spots a likely-looking meal, it moves swiftly forward. Suddenly, it stops and watches carefully for a few moments. Then it moves into cover and falls flat against the ground, ready for the final approach.

Gradually, it creeps nearer, moving more slowly, until it stops very close to the prey. Just at the right moment it springs out of cover and seizes the unsuspecting animal with its sharp teeth and strong claws.

Jungle cats feed mostly on hares, rats, mice, lizards and birds but will also eat

and other obstacles in the jungle when their whiskers brush against them.

Indeed, they are such experts at hunting that, centuries ago, the Egyptians trained jungle cats to hunt birds for them.

Although they normally live in woodland and open country, such as plains,

frogs and snakes when they are especially hungry. Although they can be seen wandering around in broad daylight, most of their hunting is done at night. They have excellent eyesight and are also able to find their way in the dark using their whiskers. They can feel trees

patches of long grass, reed beds and sugar plantations, jungle cats sometimes also prowl around villages and small towns. They are found throughout the Middle East and Asia and choose abandoned burrows of badgers, foxes or porcupines in which to make their dens.

Clouded leopard

Clouded leopards are found in some of the wildest and most inaccessible parts of the world. They live only in a few dense forests of China and some neighboring countries, where they are extremely rare and hardly ever seen.

They rest during the day – and often for much of the night – spending most of their time in the trees, where they feel most at home. They can even clamber upside-down on the underside of branches or run down trees head-first.

Hunting usually begins at twilight, when the clouded leopards creep around the forests in search of birds, monkeys, squirrels, pigs, cattle, deer or even porcupines. Sometimes they spring from a tree onto their unsuspecting prey, or may creep up and swat it with a broad, spoon-shaped paw.

The clouded leopard's coat, covered with spectacular circles, ovals and rosettes, is one of the most beautiful in the world. But the young animals are virtually black when they are first born. They do not grow coats like their parents' until they are about six months old.

Leopard cat

In China, the handsome leopard cat is affectionately known as the "money cat". Its beautifully spotted coat makes it look as if it is covered with Chinese coins.

But no two leopard cats look exactly the same. In fact, their colors and markings vary so much that scientists once thought that there were many different kinds. However, the animals that mistakenly became known as Sumatran cats, lesser cats, Javan cats and Chinese cats are all really leopard cats.

About the size of a domestic tabby, the leopard cat is one of the most common cats of southern Asia. It is found in India, Siberia, China and several other countries, where it mostly lives in forests and jungles. Since it is not particularly frightened of people, it frequently enters villages to prey on chickens and geese. An extremely graceful and elegant animal, it makes the resident house cat look almost clumsy in comparison.

Leopard cats hunt on the ground as well as in the trees. They are superb climbers and quite happily chase squirrels and birds along the thinnest of branches. They are also excellent swimmers and have managed to reach many offshore islands. There they have been able to set up home safe from the pressures of competition from other wild cats, which cannot so easily get across the water separating the islands from the mainland.

Flat-headed cat

The flat-headed cat is a rather peculiar animal because it really does have a flat head. It also has a thick, soft coat and a long body with short legs and a short tail. Indeed, at a quick glance it looks more like a mink or a polecat than a wild cat.

Flat-headed cats only come out at night and are extremely rare animals. They are found exclusively in the jungles of Malaysia, Sumatra and Borneo, where they hide in the thick undergrowth near rivers, lakes and swamps. Hardly anyone has ever seen a flat-headed cat in the wild, so very little is known about them. Practically the only thing known about the kittens is that they seem to enjoy playing in water.

The adults have been seen hunting for frogs, fish and crabs along river banks – and they have special teeth for seizing their slippery prey. They are also particularly fond of fruit, and have been known to dig up and eat sweet potatoes in people's gardens. Unlike most cats, however, they usually ignore sparrows and other birds, even if they are feeding or flitting around nearby.

Scottish wildcat

In the highlands of Scotland lives a wildcat which looks remarkably similar to a domestic tabby. It is slightly larger than its cousin and has a short thick bushy tail. But otherwise the two are almost identical. The Scottish wildcat even has a "meow" like a domestic cat and purrs when it is happy.

Wildcats are also found in central and southern Europe, right across into Asia. They live on the edge of woodlands and forests, on hill ground and grouse moors, and in rocky country. Most of the time they live alone, spending their days sleeping, then hunting at dusk and dawn for mice, voles, rabbits, hares and birds.

They build dens among rocks or under tree stumps; or, very occasionally, they use large birds' nests. The kittens are born in May but do not emerge to see the outside world until they are about four or five weeks old. At first, they spend many hours every day playing with their mother. After about three months, they begin to go out on hunting trips with her. This is important because, very soon, when they are just five months old, they will have to leave the family and look after themselves.

Wildcats do not like the rain – they usually shelter during a downpour – but love to sunbathe on sunny days. They can swim and climb well, though normally spend most of the time with their feet firmly on the ground.

Spanish lynx

When prowling around in its forest and scrubland home, the Spanish lynx is always alert. It can see and hear extremely well and can always tell when danger is approaching. Then it quickly hides, crouching down in the nearest cover until the danger has passed. Because of this habit, and because the Spanish lynx is active mostly at night, it is very rarely seen.

It is also rarely heard. Only during the breeding season is its presence given away, with strange purring and wailing sounds. These are made by the males fighting in the middle of the night over females. Noisy skirmishes and fights like these are common.

The young animals are

born in a hollow log, in a cave or under a rock. They stay there for the first few weeks of their lives, only appearing outside to practice stalking and catching prey. They usually remain with their mother during the first winter and do not live alone until the following spring.

The adults have their own special footpaths which they use on hunting trips. They often walk along them for hours on end without getting tired, searching mostly for rabbits, but also sometimes for partridges, mice and other animals. Quietly crawling along the ground, they keep their bodies as flat as possible, until they are close enough to spring out.

Although the Spanish lynx could once be found all over Spain, it is now an endangered species and only occurs in a few scattered mountainous areas.

Ocelot

In the humid jungles of Central America, the dense forests of Brazil, the bush country of Texas and other parts of America, lives a rare and very beautiful cat. Little more than half the size of a jaguar, the ocelot rarely shows itself in completely open country. It prefers to stay where there is plenty of cover and good places to hide. The dappled light of a forest is ideal, for there its spotted coat is difficult to see.

Ocelots spend the daytime sleeping in hollow trees, hidden in thick vegetation or perched on a safe branch. They come out at night to hunt for mice, rabbits, guinea pigs, young deer and snakes. Most of to live in pairs but during their night-time prowls usually hunt alone, always keeping in touch with one another by calling back and forth.

these are captured along man-made paths, which are their favorite hunting grounds. However, since they can swim and climb well, ocelots also catch fish and monkeys or birds. They tend

Ocelot kittens are born at almost any time of the year, concealed in a hollow tree or thicket. No two ocelots look exactly the same; when they grow up they all have slightly different patterns on their coats.

Margay

The very rare margay looks rather like a small ocelot, with a long tail and very large eyes, but it acts more like a monkey. It is the most acrobatic cat in the world. Also called the long-tailed spotted cat, it is a pure forest animal and spends most of its time in the trees.

Margays are effortless climbers. They run up and down tree trunks like squirrels, can hang underneath the branches like sloths and sometimes even dangle by their feet like trapeze artists.

Found from northern Mexico through Central America to northern Argentina and Uruguay, they hunt mostly in the treetops. There they chase squirrels, opossums, monkeys, birds and tree frogs with such skill and speed that their prey hardly stands a chance.

Unlike other cats, margays often jump into the air from great heights, landing with an enormous crash but, somehow, unharmed. As they jump, they spread all four legs out to the sides. If just one paw strikes

a branch, that is enough for them to grab a firm hold with their claws and stop their fall. Then they simply haul themselves up and continue on their journey.

Jaguarundi

The jaguarundi is one of the world's experts at picking its way through dense tangled undergrowth. Its short legs and slender body help it to slip through bushes, long grass and thickets with ease.

In many ways, jaguarundis look a bit like otters; as a result, they are sometimes called otter cats. They are very lively and playful animals, often chirping excitedly like birds or purring when they feel in a playful mood. They inhabit forest edges, nearly always near water, in the southern United States, Mexico, Central America and much of South America.

Unlike most cats, jaguarundis are not particularly active at night. The whole of the night and the middle of the day are spent sleeping in a den. They prefer to hunt in the morning

and evening, looking mostly for birds, mice and voles. In many parts of their range they have become very popular with farmers as important rodent exterminators. They hunt mostly on the ground and, while they are able to climb trees, do not like going too high.

A jaguarundi litter contains up to four kittens. Like their parents, they have a variety of coats, including a range from black to brown, gray or even fox-red. It is not uncommon for a single litter to have one kitten of each color.

Jaguar

The largest cat in America is the jaguar. Found from the southern United States to northern Argentina, it lives in jungles, forests, savannas, marshes, grasslands and, occasionally, scrub country.

Jaguars are excellent swimmers and like to live near lakes and rivers, where they sometimes "fish" for their food. They gently splash the tip of their tail onto the surface of the water and, when a fish rises to inspect the lure, quickly scoop it up. But they are powerful cats and can capture wild pigs, capybaras (which are like giant guinea pigs), tapirs, alligators and other large animals. These are usually stalked or ambushed on the ground but jaguars are

confident climbers and will often wait high in the branches of a tree before dropping silently onto them from above.

No one knows exactly how many jaguars are left in the wild – but their numbers have certainly declined in recent years – because so many have been killed for their attractive coats. They are most active at dusk and dawn, or during the night, and usually hunt on their own. During the daytime, however, it is sometimes possible to hear their roaring, which sounds like a loud cough, or to see them sunning themselves on a wide branch, high above the ground.

Cougar

Found all over North and South America, the cougar is famous for its high jumps. It can leap over fifteen feet from the ground into a tree, using its long and graceful tail to keep balance when it lands.

Cougars live in mountainous forests, jungles, swamps, grasslands and dry bush country. They are particularly fond of remote areas, with steep cliffs and deep canyons. Active both at night and during the day, they travel long distances and sometimes wander several hundred miles every week.

Also called pumas, panthers or mountain lions, cougars hunt mostly deer but they also sometimes catch beavers, porcupines, hares and other animals. If they are too full to eat everything at once, they cover the leftovers with leaves and debris for future meals.

Most of the time cougars live alone. They rarely sleep

in a fixed den, preferring to use temporary shelters in long grass, bushes, rocky crevices or caves. The only time they are really settled is when they have kittens, which are born in the spring. But by winter, only six months later, the kittens are hunting on their own and able to look after themselves, so the cougars are alone once again.

Bobcat

Loud screams, hisses and other eerie sounds can sometimes be heard at night coming from the forests and mountainous areas of southern Canada, the United States and Mexico. They are made by bobcats, otherwise shy and secretive animals that spend most of their time quietly avoiding one another. Only during the breeding season do they really make their presence known, with this strange calling.

Bobcats eat small animals such as jack rabbits, kangaroo rats, pocket gophers and chipmunks. They sometimes also enter caves to catch bats.

Although smaller than lynxes, bobcats look very similar with the same ruff of fur on their cheeks giving the appearance of sideburns. In some ways they are also rather like domestic cats. For example, they sleep curled up and love to sunbathe, if they can find a safe warm spot. One enormous difference, however, is that they happily soak themselves in water, which is something very few domestic cats would ever do.